A LITTLE BOOK OF FLOWERS
lore, customs, and language

Dale Evva Gelfand

*The mission of Storey Publishing is to serve our customers
by publishing practical information that encourages personal independence
in harmony with the environment.*

Edited by Deborah Balmuth and Jennifer Travis Donnelly
Cover design by Wendy Palitz
Cover illustrations © Juliette Borda
Flower illustrations by Mallory Lake, pages 50 and 53; Laura Tedeschi, page 62
Text production by Jennifer Jepson Smith

Copyright © 2002 by Storey Publishing, LLC

The information in this book is true and complete to the best of our knowledge. All recommendations are made without guarantee on the part of the author or Storey Publishing. The author and publisher disclaim any liability in connection with the use of this information. For additional information, please contact Storey Publishing, 210 MASS MoCA Way, North Adams, MA 01247.

Storey books are available for special premium and promotional uses and for customized editions. For further information, please call 1-800-793-9396.

Printed in the United States by Lake Book
10 9 8 7 6 5 4 3 2 1

ISBN 1-58017-564-3

Flowers speak to us in many ways. They symbolize joy and abundance at weddings; they convey sadness and loss at funerals; they express love and devotion at any time. From the beginning of recorded history, flowers have wordlessly expressed our emotions and thoughts.

The symbolism of flowers transcends cultural boundaries and different eras. The blue lotus, for example, which dates back to the Jurassic period some 160 million years ago, has been esteemed by many cultures for thousands of years. To the Chinese, it was a symbol of feminine beauty and represented divine female fertility. In India, Brahma, the creator of the universe, was believed to have sprung from a lotus blossom, and ancient Egyptians believed that the lotus symbolized the origin of life and that its perfume was a manifestation of the great god Ra's sweat.

Ancient Greeks and Romans used flowers as symbols of human characteristics, and many of their gods and goddesses are associated with particular blossoms. Roses are symbolic of the goddesses of love, both the Greek Aphrodite and the Roman Venus. Anemone was a Greek nymph who was turned into a flower by Flora, the jealous goddess of flowers. Peoples as widely diverse as the Aztecs and the Celts believed in the "flowered word," and the Japanese have their own term for it: *hanakotoba*. And, of course, the Bible makes numerous references to flowers and their significance.

The language of flowers as the Western world knows it today is believed to have originated in Constantinople, now

Istanbul, in present-day Turkey. However, some historians identify its birthplace as Persia, from where it traveled to Sweden — although just how this transfer occurred has not

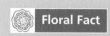

Floral Fact

Marigolds were once used to give cheese its yellow color. And the flowers were sometimes dried and used in broth.

been determined. What is definite is that Elizabethan English society was well versed in the symbolic and legendary meanings of flowers (Shakespeare freely sprinkled floral symbolism throughout his works), and the tradition of imbuing flowers with particular meanings related to human emotions spread throughout Europe. The first flower dictionary was composed by Mme. Charlotte de la Tour in 1818. Her *Le Language des Fleurs* was an overnight sensation.

It was the Victorians, however, who were most fluent in the language of flowers and raised that language to the status of a cultural phenomenon. In 1879, a Miss Corruthers of

Inverness wrote a book on *floriography* — the assigning of meanings to flowers — which became the standard for floral symbolism in both Great Britain and the United States. Victorian ladies and gentlemen — today themselves symbols of repressed emotions — could convey their feelings while still preserving the strict mores and etiquette of their society. This silent, coded language was a vehicle for the expression of wishes and thoughts, enabling people to communicate emotions not usually permitted by the propriety of the era. This "lexicon" was especially popular among lovers, requited and otherwise. (Edith Wharton used this coded language in her 1920 novel *The Age of Innocence*, and if her readers understood it, they had a far better understanding of the book's characters and their mute communications.) Indeed, not only did each flower have a particular meaning, but the arrangements and presentations of flowers were equally significant, with particular combinations of flora used to convey various subtle or overt feelings.

A suitor, for example, could present the object of his affection with a "tussie-mussie," or nosegay, consisting of gardenias, alstromeria, red carnations, snowdrops, lavender, and pansies. Understanding the language of flowers, his lady would know that he was declaring his secret love, devotion, admiration, hope, and constancy, and that she was always in his thoughts. However, if yellow chrysanthemums were added to the mix, that would mean she was always in his thoughts because his love had been slighted. Or perhaps he would send a message of esteem by giving a bouquet of mimosa, lilacs, pale-pink roses, white camellias, and yellow tulips, which might well make her blush to know that he thought her to be sensitive, enchanting, graceful, and adorable, and to have a smile like sunshine. Add a red carnation, and she would know that his heart was breaking for want of her.

On the other hand, love that had soured might result in a floral poison-pen letter consisting of foxglove (insincerity), yellow roses (infidelity), abatina (fickleness), Indian pinks (aversion), asphodel (regret), and yellow carnations (disdain and rejection). But all might not be lost. A remorseful swain could attempt to make amends with a gift consisting of purple hyacinth ("I am sorry; please forgive me"), white roses ("I hope I am worthy of you"), primroses ("I can't live without you"), and lemon blossoms ("I promise to be true").

Most of this covert language has is long forgotten; however, to this day we "say it with flowers" when we seek to express love, celebrate a joyous occasion, cheer up a sick friend, or grieve for a lost dear one.

 Floral Fact

Sunflowers, which are so named because their heads follow the sun through the course of the day, were ground into flour by Native Americans and used as a food source. And the seeds were considered a sacred food to the Plains Indians, who placed bowls filled with them on the graves of their dead to nourish them in their journey to the afterlife.

The Lure of the Rose

When the famed Scottish poet Robert Burns wrote "*O, my luve is like a red, red rose, That's newly sprung in June. . . .*" in 1797, he was a Robbie-come-lately to the spell of the rose. For eons the rose had been linked with love and romance — as well as war and politics.

Some 35 million years old today, the rose was first cultivated about 5000 years ago, probably in northern Persia. From there, it spread across Mesopotamia and Babylon — King Nebuchadrezzar II, around 600 B.C., decorated his palace with roses — to Greece. Greek legend had it that the rose sprang from the blood of Adonis, the beloved of Aphrodite, goddess of love. The word rose comes from the Latin *rosa,* which itself comes from the Greek *rodon* (red), for the deep crimson color of roses in antiquity. The blossom is mentioned in both the *Iliad* and the *Odyssey,* and Sappho, the Greek poetess who wrote around 600 B.C., declared the rose to be the queen of flowers. Pliny the Elder was a later Greek gardener who both admired and cultivated the blooms.

The ancient Romans (who, like the Greeks, created love stories for many of their favorite flowers) named the rose for Rhodanthe, whose exquisite beauty incensed the goddess Diana. In a fit of pique, Diana turned Rhodanthe into a rose and her numerous suitors into thorns. However, another myth has Cupid carrying a vase of nectar to the gods on Mount Olympus; when he stumbles and spills the nectar, the droplets spring up as roses. The rose was sacred to Bacchus, the Roman god of wine, and to Venus, the goddess of love. Paying homage to these deities during banquets in their honor, Romans draped garlands of roses around their necks, festooned their couches with rose petals, and dropped rose petals from the ceiling. Rose petals were used in such abundance at these extravagant feasts that at least one account tells of guests being suffocated by falling rose petals. Roman brides and grooms were crowned with roses to celebrate their union. The rose is dedicated to Harpocrates, the god of silence, and it is widely believed that the term *sub rosa* — literally, "under the rose" in Latin — refers back to the Roman rule that anything uttered under a hanging garland of roses was to be kept in strictest confidence. Indeed, Roman mythology has it that Cupid bribed Harpocrates with a rose to keep him from revealing Venus's many love affairs.

The ancient Egyptians, too, Cleopatra chief among them, were enchanted by roses. Whenever Cleopatra's lover Marc Antony visited, roses were strewn knee deep on the palace floors, the couches were covered in rose petals, and rose water poured from the fountains. Rose petals were routinely scattered beneath the chariot wheels of victorious soldiers, and the prows of victorious vessels were adorned with rose garlands.

Because the rose was long associated with debauchery, early Christians refused to allow roses in church. However, after the fall of the Roman Empire, rose cultivation was taken up by Benedictine monks and the rose became both the emblem of Christianity and a symbol of the Virgin Mary. At the same time, followers of Islam celebrated the rose as a symbol of perfection, and roses were widely cultivated throughout the Islamic empire, from Spain to India.

During the Middle Ages, the War of the Roses was so named because each of the factions vying for the throne of England displayed a rose as its symbol: a white rose for the House of York and a red rose for the House of Lancaster. Soon after, when Queen Elizabeth I succeeded to the throne, she regularly wore a rose tucked behind her ear — perhaps to signify that she could keep a secret.

At some point near the turn of the 17th century, the oil of roses — originally *otto of roses* but corrupted to *attar of roses* — was discovered by the Persians. At a wedding feast celebrating the marriage between a princess and the emperor, a canal was dug and filled with rose water. The sun heated the water, causing the essential oil to separate out, and when the oil was skimmed off the surface of the water, it was found to be a magnificent perfume. Soon rose-oil distilleries were contributing greatly to the empire's economy. In Europe, meanwhile, roses were held in such high esteem that they were considered legal tender and were often used as barter for payments.

In 1792, a new hybrid rose was introduced to Europe from China. Until then, roses had bloomed only one a year; this Chinese "hybrid tea rose," however, was a repeat bloomer. Virtually all modern-day roses can be traced back to this ancestor.

The Victorians — lovers of all things complicated and intricate — determined that different colors, varieties, and arrangements of roses conveyed different messages to the recipients. The red rose has long been deemed the quintessential representation of love; however, other roses, too, have special meanings:

FLOWER	MEANING
Red rose	Love, passion, respect, courage
White rose	Spiritual love and purity, humility
Pink rose	Perfect happiness, grace and sweetness, joy, secret love
Pale pink rose	Friendship, admiration
Dark pink rose	Thankfulness
Dark crimson rose	Mourning
Coral rose	Desire
Lavender rose	Love at first sight, enchantment
Peach rose	Immortality, modesty
Orange rose	Fascination, enthusiasm
Yellow rose	Historic: infidelity, decrease of love Contemporary: joy, friendship, gladness

Beyond bearing the meanings of their individual colors, roses used in various color combinations convey different meanings, as well:

COLORS	MEANING
White and red	Unity
Red and yellow	Congratulations
Yellow and orange	Passionate thoughts
Pink and white	Everlasting love

Lastly, the variety and the maturity of the blossoms also signify specific sentiments:

FLOWER	SENTIMENT
Tea rose	I'll remember always
Cabbage rose	Ambassador of love
Campion rose	Only deserve my love
Carolina rose	Love is dangerous
Christmas rose	Peace and tranquility
Damask rose	Freshness
Rosebud	Beauty and youth, a heart innocent of love
Single full bloom	I love you, I still love you
Bouquet of full blooms	Gratitude
Thornless bloom	Love at first sight
Garland or crown	Beware of virtue

The rose, a herbaceous shrub found in temperate regions throughout both hemispheres of the globe, has influenced human beings for thousands of years — and is likely to continue to do so for ages to come.

Shakespeare's Flowers and Herbs

William Shakespeare liberally used flower and herb symbolism in his writing. In *Hamlet*, Ophelia utters what is perhaps the most famous example: "*Rosemary, that's for remembrance: pray you, love, remember. And there's pansies, that's for thoughts.*" However, floral symbolism can be found in a number of Shakespeare's love sonnets as well as his plays, among them *King Lear* (peonies), *A Midsummer Night's Dream* (pansies), *A Winter's Tale* (marigolds, carnations, and daffodils), *Romeo and Juliet* (roses), and *Macbeth* (hollyhocks).

Consider, in *Macbeth*, the spell being conjured up by the three witches, also known as the weird sisters, and those ingredients being tossed into their bubbling caldron: "*Eye of newt and toe of frog / Wool of bat and tongue of dog, / Adder's fork and blindworm's sting, / Lizard's leg and howlet's wing. . . ."*

Rather than being a compilation of animal parts, these ingredients are most likely the folk names of plants and flowers. Traditional sorcery refers to spell components obliquely, with the real recipe not at all resembling what the terms invoke to the uninitiated. Therefore, *tongue of dog* is likely houndstongue, an herb purported to keep dogs from barking, and *adder's fork* is adder's tongue, a fern that supposedly has healing properties.

But Shakespeare also used flower symbolism traditionally, as metaphor. Herewith are the blooms invoked by the Bard and the meanings he ascribed to them:

FLOWER	SENTIMENT OR SYMBOL
Daffodil	Regard
Daisy	Innocence
Fennel	Strength, praiseworthiness
Gilliflower	Betrothal, marriage, fidelity

FLOWER	SENTIMENT OR SYMBOL
Hyssop	Penitence, humility
Iris	Royalty
Lavender	Cleanliness, chastity
Lily (white)	Innocence, purity
Marigold	Despair and grief
Pansy	Remembrance, meditation, "love in idleness"
Rose	Love, beauty, and charm
Rosemary	Remembrance and friendship
Rue	Regret, penitence
Violet	Modesty, faithfulness
Woodbine	Fidelity in marriage
Wormwood	Bitterness

The Language of Flowers

Floral symbolism has filtered down through the ages and divergent cultures, taking metaphors from mythology, religion, and folk medicine. (Many of the symbolic meanings have been ascribed to flowers on the basis of their character and characteristics.) For every sentiment you have, there is a flower to do your talking for you. However, a word of caution if you plan to employ these lovely Cyranos: Some flowers have more than one definition, and they can be wildly divergent.

On pages 18–43 is a list of flora and their secret messages. It is up to you to decide whether to share this plant patois or not.

 Floral Fact

There are some 25,000 varieties of orchids in the world — no thanks to mankind. Orchids were collected extensively during the 1800s, and thousands of trees were cut down for the epiphytic orchids growing on their branches. One collector alone was believed to have sent hundreds of thousands of orchids home to England — where most of them promptly died.

FLOWER	SYMBOLIC MEANING
Abatina	Fickleness
Abecedary	Volubility
Acacia	
Rose	Friendship
White	Elegance
Yellow	Secret love
Acanthus	The fine arts, artifice
Acalia	Temperance
Achillea Millefolia	War
Aconite (Wolfsbane)	Misanthropy
Aconite, Crowfoot	Luster
Adonis, Flos	Painful recollections
Agnus Castus	Coldness, indifference
Agrimony	Gratitude
Almond	
Flowering	Stupidity, indiscretion, hope
Laurel	Perfidy
Aloe	Grief, religious superstition
Althaea Frutes (Syrian Mallow)	Persuasion
Amaranth	
Cockscomb	Foppery, affectation
Globe	Immortality, unfading love

FLOWER	SYMBOLIC MEANING
Amaryllis	Pride, timidity, splendid beauty
Ambrosia	Love returned
Amethys	Admiration
Anemone	Forsaken
Angelica	Inspiration
Angrec	Royalty
Apocynum (Dog's Vane)	Deceit
Apple Blossom	Preference, perpetual concord
Arbor Vitae	Unchanging friendship, live for me
Arum (Wake Robin)	Ardor
Ash	Grandeur
Ash-Leaved Trumpet Flower	Separation
Aspen	Lamentation
Asphodel	My regrets follow you to the grave
Aster	Elegance, daintiness
Auricula, Scarlet	Avarice
Austurtium	Splendor
Azalea	Temperance
Bachelor's Buttons	Celibacy
Balloon Flower	Unchanging love, honesty, obedience
Balm	Sympathy
Balm of Gilead	Cure, relief

Flower	Symbolic Meaning
Balsam, Red	Touch me not, impatient resolves
Balsam, Yellow	Impatience
Barberry	Sourness of temper
Basil	Hatred
Bay Tree	Glory
Bay Wreath	Reward of merit
Bearded Crepis	Protection
Beech	Prosperity
Bee Ophrys	Error
Bee Orchis	Industry
Belladonna	Silence
Bell Flower	
Pyramidal . . . . Constancy	
Small White . . . . Gratitude	
Belvedere	I declare against you
Betony	Surprise
Bilberry	Treachery
Bindweed	
Great . . . . Insinuation	
Small . . . . Humility	
Birch	Meekness
Birdsfoot Trefoil	Revenge
Bittersweet; Nightshade	Truth

FLOWER	SYMBOLIC MEANING
Blackberry	Remorse
Black Poplar	Courage
Blackthorn	Difficulty
Bladder Nut	Frivolity, amusement
Bluebell	Constancy
Bluebottle	Delicacy
Borage	Bluntness
Borus Henricus	Goodness
Box Tree	Stoicism
Broom	Humility, neatness
Buckbean	Calm repose
Bugloss	Falsehood
Bulrush	Indiscretion, docility
Burdock	Importunity, boredom, touch me not
Buttercup	Ingratitude, childishness
Butterfly Weed	Let me go
Cacalia	Adulation
Cactus	Warmth, bravery, and endurance
Calandine, Lesser	Joys to come
Calla Lily	Magnificent beauty
Calycanthus	Benevolence
Camellia, Red	You're a flame in my heart
Camellia, White	Adoration, perfection, loveliness

FLOWER	SYMBOLIC MEANING
Canary Grass	Perseverance
Candytuft	Indifference
Canterbury Bell	Gratitude, constancy, and warning
Cape Jasmine	I'm too happy
Cardamine	Paternal error
Cardinal Flower	Distinction
Carnation	
Pink	I'll never forget you
Red	My heart aches for you, admiration
Striped	Refusal
White	Pure love, sweet love, innocence
Yellow	Disdain
Catchfly	
Red	Youthful love
White	Betrayed
Cedar	I live for thee, strength
Centaury	Delicacy
Cereus	
Creeping	Modest genius
Night-Blooming	Transient beauty
Chamomile	Energy in action, initiative and ingenuity
Champignon	Suspicion
Cherry Blossom	Nobility

FLOWER	SYMBOLIC MEANING
Chestnut Tree	Do me justice, luxury
Chickweed	Rendezvous
Chicory	Frugality
China Aster	Variety
Double	I partake your sentiments
Single	I will think of it
Chinese Chrysanthemum	Cheerfulness under adversity
Chives	Why are you crying?
Chrysanthemum	
Red	I love you, happiness
White	Truth, optimism
Yellow	Slighted love
Cinquefoil	Maternal affection
Circaea	Spell
Cistus, or Rock Rose	Popular favor
Citron	Ill-natured beauty
Clematis	Intellectual beauty, artifice, ingenuity
Clove	Dignity
Clover	
Four-leaf	Be mine
Red	Industry
White	Think of me

FLOWER	SYMBOLIC MEANING
Cobaea	Gossip
Cockscomb Amaranth	Foppery, affectation, singularity
Colchicum, or Meadow Saffron	My best days are past
Coltsfoot	Justice shall be done
Columbine	Folly, desertion
Purple	Resolved to win
Red	Anxious and trembling
Convolvulus	Bonds
Minor (Blue)	Repose
Major	Extinguished hopes
Pink	Worth sustained by judicious and tender affection
Coreopsis	Always cheerful
Coriander	Hidden worth
Cornflower	Delicacy, refinement
Cowslip	Pensiveness, winning grace, healing
Cranberry	Cure for heartache
Cress	Stability, power
Crocus	Abuse not
Saffron	Mirth
Spring	Youtful gladness
Crown Imperial	Majesty, power

FLOWER	SYMBOLIC MEANING
Crown Vetch	Success crowns your wishes
Crowfoot	Ingratitude
Crowsbill	Envy
Cuckoo	Ardor
Currant	Thy frown will kill me
Cyclamen	Diffidence, resignation, voluptuousness
Cypress	Death, mourning
Daffodil	Unrequited love, regard, chivalry
Dahlia	Gratitude, dignity, elegance
Daisy	Innocence, purity, loyal love
Gerbera	Friendship
Michaelmas	Farewell
Ox-eye	Patience
Dandelion	Rustic oracle, wishes come true
Daphane	
Rose	I desire to please
Winter	I would not have you otherwise
Daylily	Flirt, beauty
Dead Leaves	Sadness
Delphinium	Sweetness, airy
Dew Plant	A serenade
Dill	Irresistible, lust
Dock	Patience

FLOWER	SYMBOLIC MEANING
Dogsbane	Deceit, falsehood
Dogwood	Durability
Dragon Plant	Snare
Dusty Miller	Delicacy
Edelweiss	Daring, courage, noble purity
Elderberry	Humility, kindness
Elder Flower	Zealousness
Elm	Dignity
Eupatorium	Delay
Euphorbia	Persistence
Everlasting	Constancy
Fennel	Worthy all praise, strength
Fern	Fascination, sincerity
Maidenhair	Secret bond of love
Royal	Reverie
Fig	Argument
Filbert	Reconciliation
Flax	Fate, I feel your kindness
Fleur-de-Lis	Flame, I burn
Flower-of-an-Hour	Delicate beauty
Flytrap	Deceit
Fool's Parsley	Silliness
Forget-Me-Not	True love, forget me not

FLOWER	SYMBOLIC MEANING
Forsythia	Anticipation
Four O'Clock	Timidity
Foxglove	Insincerity
Freesia	Innocence
Fritillary	Persecution
Frog Ophrys	Disgust
Fuchsia, Scarlet	Amiability, confiding love
Gardenia	Secret love, purity, refinement
Gentian, Fringed	Intrinsic worth
Geranium	
Ivy	Bridal favor
Lemon	Unexpected meeting
Nutmeg	Expected meeting
Oak-leaf	Friendship
Rose-scented	Preference
Scarlet	Melancholy, consolation
Silver-leaved	Recall
Wild	Steadfast piety
Gillyflower	Bonds of affection
Gladiolus	Strength of character
Glory Flower	Glorious beauty
Gloxinia	Love at first sight
Goat's Rue	Reason

Flower	Symbolic Meaning
Goldenrod	Precaution, treasure, and good fortune
Gooseberry	Anticipation
Grape, Wild	Charity
Harebell	Submission, grief
Hawkweed	Quicksightedness
Hazel	Reconciliation

Heather
  Lavender ....Admiration, solitude
  White ....Protection from danger	

Helenium	Tears
Heliotrope	Devotion, faithfulness
Hellebore	Scandal, calumny
Helmet Flower (Monkshood)	Knight-errantry
Hemlock	You will be my death
Hemp	Fate
Henbane	Imperfection
Hepatica	Confidence
Hibiscus	Delicate beauty
Holly	Foresight
Hollyhock	Ambition, fecundity
Honesty	Honesty, fascination
Honey Flower	Love sweet and secret

Flower	Symbolic Meaning
Honeysuckle	Generous and devoted affection
Hop	Injustice
Hortensia	You are cold
Houseleek	Vivacity, domestic industry
Houstonia	Content
Hoya	Sculpture
Humble Plant	Despondence
Hyacinth	
Blue	Consistency
Purple	Please forgive me, sorrow
White	Unobtrusive loneliness
Yellow	Jealousy
Hydrangea	Boastfulness, heartlessness, frigidity
Hyssop	Cleanliness
Iceland Moss	Health
Imperial Montague	Power
Iris	Faith, wisdom, promise in love, hope, wisdom, valor
German	Flame
Yellow	Passion
Ivy	Fidelity, marriage, friendship, affection
Jacob's Ladder	Come down

FLOWER	SYMBOLIC MEANING
Jasmine	Amiability
Cape	Transport of joy
Carolina	Separation
Indian	Attachment
Spanish	Sensuality
Yellow	Modesty, grace, elegance
White	Amiability
Jonquil	Love me, have pity on my passion
Juniper	Succor, protection
Justicia	The perfection of female loveliness
Kalanchoe	Popularity
Kennedia	Intellectual beauty
Kings-Cups	Desire of riches
Laburnum	Forsaken, pensive beauty
Lady's Slipper	Capricious beauty, win me
Lagerstraemia, Indian	Eloquence
Lantana	Rigor
Larch	Audacity, boldness
Larkspur	Levity, open heart, lightness, swiftness
Pink	Fickleness
Purple	Haughtiness

FLOWER	SYMBOLIC MEANING
Laurel	Glory
Ground	Perseverance
Mountain	Ambition
Laurestinus	A token, I die if neglected
Lavender	Distrust
Lemon Blossom	Fidelity in love
Lichen	Dejection, solitude
Licorice, Wild	I declare against you
Lilac	Humility
Purple	First emotions of love
White	Youthful innocence
Lily	
Imperial	Majesty
Scarlet	High-bred
Tiger	Prosperity, pride
White	Purity, sweetness
Yellow	Gratitude, gaiety
Lily of the Valley	Sweetness, return of happiness, humility
Live Oak	Liberty
Liverwort	Confidence
Lobelia	Malevolence
Lotus	Purity, resurrection, evolution, potential

Flower	Symbolic Meaning
Lotus Leaf	Recantation
Love-in-a-Mist	Perplexity
Love Lies Bleeding	Hopeless, not heartless
Lucerne	Life
Lungwort	Thou art my life
Lupine	Voraciousness, imagination
Madder	Calumny
Magnolia	
Chinese	Love of nature
Grandiflora	Peerless and proud, dignity, splendid beauty
Swamp	Perseverance
Mallow	Mildness
Marsh	Beneficence
Syrian	Consumed by love
Venetian	Delicate beauty
Mandrake	Horror
Marigold	Sacred affection, cruelty, grief, jealousy
African	Vulgar minds
French	Jealousy
Prophetic	Prediction
Marjoram	Comfort and consolation
Marvel-of-Peru	Flame of love

FLOWER	SYMBOLIC MEANING
Meadow Saffron	My best days are past
Meadowsweet	Uselessness
Mezereon	Desire to please
Michaelmas Daisy	Afterthought
Mignionette	Your qualities surpass your charms
Milfoil	War
Milkwort	Hermitage
Milvetch	Your presence softens my pains
Mimosa (Sensitive Plant)	Sensitiveness
Mint	Virtue, passion
Mistletoe	Affection, surmounting difficulties
Mock Orange	Counterfeit
Monkshood (Helmet Flower)	Misanthropy, chivalry, knight-errantry
Moonwort	Forgetfulness
Morning Glory	Affectation
Moschatel	Weakness
Moss	Maternal love
Motherwort	Concealed love
Mourning Bride	Unfortunate attachment, I have lost all
Mouse-Ear Chickweed	Forget me not
Moving Plant	Agitation

FLOWER	SYMBOLIC MEANING
Mudwort	Tranquility
Mugwort	Happiness
Musk Plant	Weakness
Mustard Seed	Indifference
Myrobalan	Privation
Myrrh	Gladness
Myrtle	Love, joy, mirth
Narcissus	Egotism, formality
Nasturtium	Conquest, victory in battle, patriotism
Nettle, Burning	Slander
Night Convolvulus	Night
Nightshade	Truth
Oak Leaves	Bravery
Oats	The witching soul of music
Oleander	Beauty and grace, beware
Olive Branch	Peace
Orange Blossom	Innocence, eternal love, your purity equals your loveliness
Orchid	Love, beauty, refinement
Cattleya	Mature charm
Dendrobium	Lust, greed, wealth
Osier	Frankness

FLOWER	SYMBOLIC MEANING
Osmunda	Dreams
Palm	Victory
Pansy	Thoughtful remembrance
Pasque Flower	You have no claims
Passionflower	Faith and piety
Patience Dock	Patience
Peach Blossom	I am your captive, generosity
Pea, Everlasting	An appointed meeting, lasting pleasure
Pear Blossom	Affection, health, hope
Pennyroyal	Flee, go away
Peony	Shame, bashfulness, compassion
Peppermint	Warmth of feeling

Periwinkle
  Blue . . . . .Early friendship
  White . . . . .Pleasures of memory	

Persicaria	Restoration
Persimmon	Bury me amid Nature's beauties
Pheasant's Eye	Remembrance
Phlox	Unanimity
Pigeon Berry	Indifference
Pimpernel	Change, assignation
Pineapple	You are perfect

FLOWER	SYMBOLIC MEANING
Pink	Boldness
Indian, Double	Always lovely
Indian, Single	Aversion, dislike
Mountain	Aspiring
Red, Double	Pure and ardent love, sincere love
Single	Pure love
Variegated	Refusal
White	Ingeniousness, talent, you are fair
Plum Blossom	Independence
Polyanthus	Pride of riches
Crimson	The heart's mystery
Lilac	Confidence
Pomegranate, Flower	Mature elegance
Poplar	
Black	Courage
White	Time
Poppy	
Red	Consolation
Scarlet	Fantastic extravagance
White	Sleep, my bane, my antidote
Prickly Pear	Satire
Pride of China	Dissension

FLOWER	SYMBOLIC MEANING
Primrose	Youth
Evening	Inconstancy
Red	Unpatronized merit
Privet	Prohibition
Purple Clover	Provident
Pyrus Japonica	Fairies' fire
Quaking Grass	Agitation
Quamoclit	Busybody
Queen's Rocket	You're the queen of coquettes, fashion
Quince	Temptation
Ragged Robin	Wit
Ranunculus	I am dazzled by your charms
Wild	Ingratitude
Raspberry	Remorse
Red Catchfly	Youthful love
Reed	Complaisance, music
Split	Indiscretion
Rhododendron (Rosebay)	Danger, beware
Rhubarb	Advice
Rocket	Rivalry

FLOWER	SYMBOLIC MEANING
Rose	
Austrian	You are all that is lovely
Bridal	Happiness
Burgundy	Unconscious beauty
Cabbage	Ambassador of love
Campion	Only deserve my love
Carolina	Love is dangerous
China	Beauty always new
Christmas	Relieve my anxiety
Damask	Freshness
Dark Crimson	Mourning
Deep Red	Bashful shame
Dog	Pleasure and pain
Japan	Beauty is your only attraction
Maiden Blush	If you love me, you will find it out
Multiflora	Grace
Musk	Capricious beauty
Peach	Let's get together
Pink	Grace, gentility, perfect happiness
Single	Simplicity
Thornless	Love at first sight
White	Innocence, I am worthy of you
White (withered)	Transient impressions

FLOWER	SYMBOLIC MEANING
Rose *(continued)*	
Yellow	Infidelity, jealousy
York and Lancaster	War
White and Red	Unity
Rosemary	Remembrance, fidelity
Rudbeckia	Justice
Rue	Disdain
Rush	Docility
Rye Grass	Changeable disposition
Saffron	Beware of excess, do not abuse
Meadow	My happiest days are past
Sage	Domestic virtue, wisdom, long life, good health
Sage, Garden	Esteem
Salvia	Forever yours
Saxifrage, Mossy	Affection
Scabious	Unfortunate love
Scotch Fir	Elevation
Sensitive Plant	Sensibility, delicate feelings
Senvy	Indifference
Shamrock	Lightheartedness
Snapdragon	Presumption, deception, danger
Snowdrop	Hope, consolation

FLOWER	SYMBOLIC MEANING
Sorrel	Affection
Spearmint	Warmth of sentiment
Speedwell	Female fidelity
Spiderwort	Esteem but not love
Star of Bethlehem	Atonement, reconciliation, purity
Starwort	Afterthought, welcome to a stranger
Stock	Bonds of affection, you will always be beautiful to me
Stock, Ten Week	Promptness
Stonecrop	Tranquility
Straw	
Broken	Broken contract
Whole	Union
Strawflower	Agreement
Sumac	Intellectual excellence
Sunflower	
Dwarf	Adoration, loyalty
Tall	Haughtiness
Sweet Alyssum	Worth beyond beauty
Sweetbrier	
American	Simplicity
European	I wound to heal
Yellow	Decrease of love, let us forget

FLOWER	SYMBOLIC MEANING
Sweet Pea	Blissful pleasure, departure
Sweet Sultan	Felicity
Sweet William	Gallantry, finesse, and perfection
Sweet Woodruff	Humility
Syringa	Memory
Tamarisk	Crime
Tansy (Wild)	I declare war against you
Teasel	Misanthropy
Tendrils of Climbing Plants	Ties
Thistle Common	Austerity
Scotch	Retaliation
Thorn Apple	Deceitful charms
Thrift	Sympathy
Throatwort	Neglected beauty
Thyme	Activity, courage, strength, energy
Tiger Lily	Wealth, may pride befriend me
Traveler's Joy	Safety
Tree of Life	Old age
Trefoil	Revenge
Tremella	Resistance
Trillium	Modest beauty

Flower	Symbolic Meaning
Truffle	Surprise
Trumpet Flower	Fame, separation
Tuberose	Dangerous pleasures, dangerous love
Tulip (all colors)	Perfect lover, declaration of love
Red	Irresistible love
Variegated	Beautiful eyes
Yellow	Hopeless love
Tussilage, Sweet-Scented	Justice shall be done you
Valerian	
Common	Accomodating disposition
Greek	Rupture
Verbena	Pray for me, sensibility
Vernal Grass	Poor but happy
Veronica	Fidelity
Vervain	Enchantment
Vine	Intoxication
Violet	Modesty, constancy
Virgin's Bower	Filial love
Volkamenia	May you be happy
Wallflower	Fidelity in adversity

FLOWER	SYMBOLIC MEANING
Watcher-by-the-Wayside	Never despair
Water Lily	Purity of heart
Wax Plant	Susceptibility
Whortleberry	Treason
Willow Creeping .... Weeping	Love forsaken Mourning
Winter Cherry	Deception
Wisteria	Welcome
Witch Hazel	A spell
Woodbine	Fraternal love
Wood Sorrel	Joy, maternal tenderness
Wormwood	Absence, do not be discouraged
Xanthium	Rudeness, pertinacity
Xeranthemum	Eternity, immortality
Yarrow	Heals wounds
Yew	Sorrow
Zephyr Flower	Expectation, sincerity
Zinnia	Thoughts of absent friends, affection

Floral Myths and Legends

Beyond speaking their symbolic language, many of our favorite flowers have romantic (and other) myths, legends, and superstitions attached to them. Here are a few garden favorites.

Anemone

Originating in Greece and the eastern Mediterranean, this beautiful member of the buttercup family was introduced into Britain in 1596. Two differing Greek myths tell the origin of the name *anemone*. In one myth, Zephyr, god of the West Wind, was in love with a nymph, but Flora, the goddess of flowers, became enraged with jealousy and turned the nymph into a flower: the anemone. The second myth has Aphrodite, goddess of love, weeping for Adonis; born of her tears are the beautiful anemone flowers. A later legend, from Palestine, has anemones growing under the cross of Jesus.

Superstitions about anemones abound. The ancient Egyptians thought that anemones carried diseases and so made them their emblem of sickness. Similarly, the Chinese call anemones the Flower of Death. To the contrary, the Romans used anemones as a charm against fever. Peasants in some European countries, however, thought anemones were a bad omen, and it was a custom to hold one's breath when traversing an anemone field, for it was believed that even the air around the flower was poisonous.

Today, of course, the anemone is one of our most appreciated garden flowers, prized for its beautiful colors.

 Floral Fact

The bird of paradise flower, native to South Africa, is named after actual birds of paradise. These creatures are considered by many to be the most beautiful birds in the world, and the blossoms of the bird of paradise flower somewhat resemble their plumage.

Aster

The name aster is Latin for "star" (this explains the aster's other name, *starwort*), which refers both to the flower's starlike shape and the Greek legend in which Virgo scattered stardust on a field, which then bloomed with asters. Another legend maintains that the goddess Asterea cried when she looked down on the earth and saw no stars, and where her tears fell, asters bloomed. Roman mythology tells the tale of Belides, one of a group of dryads dancing at the forest's edge. When she attracted Vertumnus, the god presiding over orchards, she transformed herself into an aster to escape his pursuit.

It was long believed that when the leaves of asters were burned, the odor drove away serpents. Asters were laid on the graves of French soldiers, symbolizing the wish that events had turned out differently. Indeed, the aster is the floral symbol of France.

Today more than 600 species of asters have been culti-vated; one of the most popular is the Monte Casino.

Carnation

The original Greek name for the carnation, which was first discovered in the Far East and has been cultivated for more than 2000 years, was *dianthus*, meaning divine flower — and dianthus is still this beloved flower's botanical name. The ancient Romans called it *Jove's flower* and used it in tribute to this admired god. The ancient Greeks, too, considered the carnation their most adored flower. And according to a Christian legend, when Mary saw her beloved son carrying the cross, she wept; where her tears fell, carnations sprang up. Thus carnations, particularly pink ones, once symbolized a mother's undying love.

Floral Fact

The late Queen Victoria so believed in the language of flowers that she made sure her bridal bouquet contained myrtle, which symbolized constancy in affection and duty. She later planted some myrtle and to this day, a piece of Victoria's myrtle plant is tucked into the bride's bouquet at every British royal wedding.

Korean superstition believes in the fortune-telling properties of carnations. A cluster of three carnations placed in a girl's hair foretells her fate by their order of their death. If the top flower dies first, the girl's final years will be difficult ones. If the middle flower dies first, her early years will be the most unhappy. And if the bottom flower dies first, she will be miserable the whole of her life. Carnations have also been thought to have medicinal properties. During the 13th century, Crusaders stricken with the plague drank a concoction of carnation leaves mixed with wine to control raging fevers. Later, botanist John Gerard wrote in his 16th-century herbal that carnation flowers mixed to a conserve with sugar would expel poison and fevers.

Daffodil

Daffodils are also known as jonquil and narcissus. According to Greek mythology, Narcissus was a youth on whom the gods had bestowed great beauty, and a wood nymph named Echo fell in love with him. Though she warned him not to look at his own reflection, Narcissus was so enamored of his looks that he completely ignored Echo, who so languished for her self-absorbed lover that she faded away until all that was left was her voice. Furious, the goddess Nemesis led Narcissus to a shimmering lake, where he leaned too far over to gaze at his reflection and drowned. Thinking this sentence a bit harsh, the gods turned the youth into a flower, the narcissus.

The flower was thought unlucky by poultry keepers, who would not grow it in their gardens or allow daffodil blossoms in their houses for fear that their chickens would stop laying or the eggs wouldn't hatch. The Chinese, however, believe that the flower brings good luck for the whole year if it's forced to bloom during the New Year. (Whether this works only for the Chinese New Year or for the Western New Year as well is not known — but this may be the origin of the modern American custom of planting and forcing daffodil bulbs indoors during the winter.)

Although the ancient Greeks associated daffodils with death — according to a myth, daffodils grew in the meadows of the Underworld, the kingdom of the dead — the Romans believed that daffodil sap could heal wounds. (In actual fact, the sap contains sharp crystals that irritate the skin.) The American Cancer Society has sided with the Roman tradition of ascribing healing powers to this flower and, believing that it symbolizes new hope and life, has adopted the daffodil as a symbol of the search for a cure for cancer.

Daisy

Daisies — actually, chrysanthemums — go as far back as civilization itself. Four-thousand-year-old gold hairpins with daisylike ornaments were found in the excavation of the Minoan palace, and images of daisies were inscribed on Egyptian ceramics. The Ancient Greeks dedicated the daisy to Artemis, goddess of women. According to the ancient Celts, daisies came from the sprits of children who died at birth; to cheer up the bereaved parents, the gods sprinkled these charming flowers all over the earth. Apparently the Celtic people later decided daisies were a pest rather than a delight, because the Scots appointed riders to remove daisies from their wheat fields, and the farmer found to have the biggest remaining daisy crop had to pay a fine consisting of a castrated ram.

Medicinally, because of the flower's eyelike center, the Assyrians believed that daisies cured eye troubles. (They also mixed crushed daisies with oil to dye gray hair dark.) During the Middle Ages, it was believed that ingesting small doses of crushed daisies steeped in wine over 15 days would cure insanity, and daisies were also used to treat smallpox, jaundice, skin diseases, tumors, inflammation of the liver, and "alle the iwarde parts." The daisy was an ingredient in a 14th-century ointment used for wounds, gout, and fevers. King Henry VIII ate daisies to relieve the pain of his stomach ulcers. Eating daisy roots would supposedly stunt a child's growth, but that same child could ensure that he would never have another toothache by eating three daisy blossoms after a tooth extraction.

Daisies have long factored in superstitions, the most famous, of course, being the ritual of pulling off the petals to learn whether your beloved loves you or loves you not. Another superstition declares that if a girl shuts her eyes and plucks a bunch of daisies, the number of blooms she has grabbed foretells how many years she has until she marries. English milkmaids believed that placing daisy roots under their pillows would induce dreams of love. And while dreaming of daisies during spring would mean good luck, the same dream would bring bad luck in fall.

Foxglove

Associated with magic, foxglove — the name comes from the Anglo-Saxon foxes' glove — was given by fairies to foxes to wear as gloves to prevent them from getting caught while raiding chicken coops. Another legend has foxes begging God for protection against the hunters who would kill them for their bushy tails, which were used as a charm against the devil. Being merciful, God put the bell-shaped flowers in fields so that they would ring whenever hunters approached.

Folk names for foxglove are *fairy thimbles* (Ireland) and *goblin's glove* (Wales). One superstition tells that picking foxglove offends the fairies. However, if fairies steal your baby, the juice of the foxglove will ensure the baby's return.

Medicinally, the ancient Greeks and Romans used the juice to heal sprains and bruises. Medieval witches used the chemical digitalis in foxglove as a potent ingredient in their spells to cause sudden death. This same chemical is, of course, recognized today as a beneficial drug for cardiac disease. Foxglove was also used to treat dropsy, stimulating the kidneys to release excessive fluid accumulated in the body.

Foxglove is prized for its many hybrids as well as for the wildflower that liberally self-seeds in shaded areas.

Iris

This beautiful flower is named for Iris, the Greek goddess of the rainbow, who was a messenger on Mount Olympus, the home of the gods. She carried messages from the eye of heaven down to earth on the arc of the rainbow. Iris was also responsible for transporting the souls of women to the Elysian Fields, and Greek men would plant an iris on the graves of their departed women. Because it was a symbol of power and majesty, the iris was dedicated to the Roman goddess Juno, wife of Jupiter. The ancient Egyptians also viewed the iris as a symbol of power, going so far as to inscribe it on the brow of the Sphinx, and in 1479 B.C. King Thutmose III had irises drawn on the walls of his temple to commemorate his victory over Syria. The three leaves of the iris were believed to symbolize faith, wisdom, and valor, and both ancient Indians and ancient Egyptians used the iris in their art to represent life and resurrection. The Catholic church later adopted the iris as an emblem of the Virgin Mary, and the three petals have been used to represent the Holy Trinity.

Since the 13th century the iris has symbolized France. The fleur-de-lis was originally "fleur-de-Louis," after Louis VI, the first French monarch to use the iris on his shield. The name was corrupted to "fleur-de-luce" (flower of light) before ending up in its current form, "fleur-de-lis" (flower of the lily). Also known as "flags," irises relate to heraldry, and in Japan they express heroism.

Medicinally, the iris was thought by the Greeks to have healing powers — it was, after all, a sacred flower — and it was used against coughs, colds, indigestion, and sciatica. Iris root has been exploited for its cathartic and emetic properties. The Greeks and Romans also cultivated iris roots for use in perfumery, and the Macedonians concocted unguents from irises.

Lily

The lily was an important flower to virtually every ancient civilization. It was the sacred flower of the Minoans, who believed it to be a special attribute of their great goddess Britomartis, who dates back to the Neolithic period. The cult of Britomartis was assimilated by the Greeks, and she became the precursor of their goddess Artemis. In Roman times, the lily was dedicated to the supreme goddess Hera, wife of Zeus. It seems that Zeus drugged his wife to have her nurse his baby born of a mortal woman — so that the infant could more fully enjoy divinity — and when Hera awoke and was horrified to find the child at her breast, she flung the baby from her. Some of her milk splashed across the heavens, creating the Milky Way, but a few drops fell to earth, and from them lilies sprang up.

The lily was also popular in the ancient Jewish culture, and it is frequently mentioned in the Old Testament. The

Chinese defined the lily as the symbol of abundance. On the flip side, the Madonna lily — until the 16th century the only variety known — symbolizes purity to the Christian church. Considered the special flower of the Virgin Mary, the lily became the symbol of chastity and virtue. Ironically, in both Christian and pagan traditions, the lily also represents fertility.

Folklore tells that lilies spontaneously appear on the graves of people who have been executed for crimes that they didn't commit. And Spaniards once believed that eating lily petals would restore the human form of someone turned into a beast.

Superstition holds that dreaming of lilies in spring foretells marriage, happiness, and prosperity, but dreaming of them in winter spells frustration of hope and the untimely death of a loved one. The Ancient Romans were said to have cured corns with the juice from lily bulbs.

Poppy

According to the ancient Romans, Somnus, the god of sleep, created the poppy to help Ceres, the goddess of agriculture. Apparently Ceres was so worn out from searching for her lost daughter that she couldn't make the corn grow. The poppies soothed her to sleep (these were no doubt opium poppies), and when she awoke refreshed, the corn grew again. (Meanwhile, her Greek counterpart, Demeter, was apparently having the same problem sleeping after the loss of *her* daughter, Persephone.) Poppies have been found in 3000-year-old Egyptian tombs, and the Chinese and Indians have cultivated poppies for centuries.

Early Romans also used poppies for witchcraft because they believed they would ease the pain of love. The Greeks thought that poppies were a sign of fertility and used them as a love charm. Christianity put a different spin on the somnambulant properties of the flower. Medieval church fathers often had the blossom carved into pews to represent the belief that we rest in anticipation of the Judgment Day.

The Ancient Greeks believed that poppy seeds brought health and strength, so athletes were given mixtures of poppy seeds, honey, and wine. Today, of course, morphine and codeine are two important drugs derived from poppies.

 Floral Fact

Chrysanthemums are cherished by Asian cultures, which consider them to be sacred flowers. The Japanese, who brought the chrysanthemum plant from China, embellish the imperial coat of arms with a golden chrysanthemum, and Japanese emperors once sat upon chrysanthemum thrones. The Chinese consider the chrysanthemum one of the four "noble plants," the others being the plum, orchid, and bamboo. According to the practice of feng shui, chrysanthemums bring happiness to your home.

Violet

The gentle little violet came to life in a most violent way, according to legend. The Phyrigian mother of the gods, Cybele, loved a shepherd named Attis. He was gored by a boar and bled to death beneath a pine tree. Violets were said to have sprung from the drops of his blood. So beloved were violets by the Greeks that they figured prominently in other myths. A nymph named Lo was adored by Zeus, who changed her into a white cow to hide her from his vengeful wife, Hera. When Lo cried over the taste of the coarse grass she had to eat, Zeus changed her tears into sweet-smelling violets that only she was allowed to graze on. In another tale, Persephone, daughter of earth mother Demeter, was gathering violets with her friends when Pluto spied her, fell instantly in love with her, and carried her off to live with him in Hades. The Romans, too, had their violet legends. According to one, Venus created the flower after a dispute with her son Cupid over who was more beautiful, herself or a bevy of other girls. When Cupid declared the girls the fairest, Venus went into a rage and beat the girls, turning them blue — and into violets.

Violets have been associated prominently with death. The ancient Greeks threw them into graves in such quantities that they completely concealed the body therein. In England, too, violets were thrown into graves to signify remembrance. And Welsh superstition held that if a man had been beaten, one could divine whether he would survive by binding a bruised violet to his forefinger. If the man fell asleep, he would recover; if he stayed awake, he would die. (To the contrary, however, a 10th-century English herbal promised that the blossoms would chase away evil spirits.)

On the flip side, violets were used as a cosmetic by the ancient Britons, and Celtic women concocted a beauty lotion by mixing violets and goat's milk. The violet plant also happens to contain salicylic acid, the primary ingredient in aspirin, and violets have been used medicinally from the 1500s onward. They have even been used as a food source. When invading Tartars traveled westward across the steppes of Russia and had to live off the land, they cooked down the roots of violets into a thick soup, sating their hunger. Violets are still eaten today — their sugar content makes them a natural to crystallize and serve as candy or pastry decorations.